HEALINGS I HAVE WITNESSED THE LORD PERFORM

John E. Burchell

ISBN 978-1-63885-998-7 (Paperback)
ISBN 978-1-63885-999-4 (Digital)

First Edition

Covenant Books, Inc.
11661 Hwy 707
Murrells Inlet, SC 29576
www.covenantbooks.com

CONTENTS

INTRODUCTION

I am writing this because as I look back over my time in ministry, which is still in progress, it is amazing to me the number of healings of different aspects of life I have witnessed and been allowed by my Lord to be involved in. When I look back and ponder the ups and the downs of ministry, it never ceases to astound me the wondrous things my Lord has done right in front of many people, and yet some of those same people still have a problem in believing that their Lord will heal them.

I was asked one time by a lady who is of a different denomination the question, "What do you do when you realize that you have a health issue?" She went on to say she was not talking about something that was necessarily a catastrophe, even though that would count as a health issue, but more like the day-to-day things each one of us experience health-wise in our lives. Her point was, do you think about going to the doctor to get your diagnosis and probably a prescription, or do you go to a quiet place in your home and go to the Lord Jesus in prayer for your diagnosis and healing?

I was shocked when I looked at myself and really examined my life and the health issues I've had and what my answer truly happened to be. I discovered that in my life, virtually every time I have a health-related issue, I would go to a medical doctor for my diagnosis and for my relief or cure. This really shocked me because at the time I was asked this question, I was smack-dab in the middle of my ministry as pastor of a denominational church.

The results of my pondering the question hit me pretty hard, and I recounted several instances in the Bible where Jesus was with His disciples and he made the statement, *"You of little faith!"* I discovered that I was one of those. Even though I studied the Bible and the words of God, when it came to my health, I normally always went to see my medical doctor, instead of my Lord. Do not take this statement wrong because I do believe that doctors are used by my Lord to help us and to do things, we need done in our lives concerning our health, but I do not really believe they should be the first person we seek out when we have an ailment that affects our health and wellbeing.

In this writing, I am going to explore some of the instances where I have witnessed, and in most of these cases, I was a part of the process that brought my Lord into the equation, a person was healed in a miraculous way. I hope and pray that this writing will help you, the reader, to look at your life, especially when it comes to your physical and spiritual health and where you go first for your help and healing.

I need to tell you, the reader, that even though the places and the names of the places may be correct, the names of the individuals in the chapters are totally fictional. Any casual similarity to the actual person is purely accidental. These things do not change in any way the content of the story or the actual action by my Lord and Savior, Jesus Christ.

MY BEGINNING LEADING TO MY MINISTRY

Most people have a preconceived idea that pastors are born pastors, and their lives, from birth to when they actually become a pastor, is nothing but one blessing after another. I am here to tell you that could not be further from the truth, especially in my particular case. I was born in Wichita, Kansas, in 1947, and I have one sister from my mother's marriage to my father. Shortly after our births, my mother went through a divorce that was less than pleasant, but she stayed the course and played the hand she was dealt.

With two babies, she had no choice but to go to work and do everything she could to provide her children with a place to live, food to eat, and clothes to wear. She was lucky because we were surrounded by family that helped with the watching of us while mother was at work and with some financial help, especially when my sister or myself became ill and needed to go to a doctor. We lived in a small rented house, which had a small kitchen with eating area, a bedroom and a bathroom, and a small front room or living room. There were only three of us in this small but adequate home, but it was warm and filled with a mother's love.

Mother did not have a car because she could not afford one, so she would take the city bus to where she worked or within a block of where she worked, and then she would walk the rest of the way. When she rode the city bus home at night, she would be within a half block of our house since it was basically right in the middle of the block. Mother would get my sister and me up in the mornings before she had to leave to catch the city bus, feed us some cereal, then drop us off at our aunt and uncle's house at the end of the block, right by the bus stop. This was the way we lived for a couple of years.

Then my mother met a man. I believe he worked at the same place she did. They had some sort of romance, and finally they were married; now there were four of us in the little rented house, but things were about to change. Our new father found a different job, and we were able to move into a much larger home with two bedrooms, a huge front or living room, big kitchen with large eating area, and a basement. I do not know what I thought about all of this. After all, what does a kid of six or seven think about things like the size of the house in which he lives? I was well fed, loved, cared for, with clean clothes to wear. What more could a kid ask for?

My introduction to "church" was when I was about six years of age, and my aunt and uncle, who were members of the First Christian Church in Wichita, Kansas, started taking me and my sister to church with them on Sundays. My mother would get us up out of bed and make sure we were dressed in clean clothes before my aunt and uncle would come by in their car to pick us up and take us with them to church. I remember they would give us each a quarter and tell us we were to place that quarter in the offering plate when it was passed by us in the pew.

I did not really understand why I was to put this quarter in the offering plate, but because I saw my uncle place money into the offering plate, I just followed his action and would place my quarter in the plate also. I do not remember anyone ever telling me why we did this, so I just thought it was some sort of payment for allowing us to come to the church on Sunday mornings and be a part of the service.

This Sunday church thing with my aunt and uncle continued for a long time, as I recall, but in reality, it was just something we did with my aunt and uncle on Sunday. The thing I remember most about the Sunday experience was the fact that we went to my aunt and uncle's house after church for a great dinner. There were no slow cookers in those days, but my aunt was a really good cook, and she would have something in the oven that would be ready when we returned home from church.

Notice that I tell you about my aunt and uncle taking my sister and me to church; I do not ever remember my mother or my dad ever going to church on Sunday. I never remember throughout my childhood or my entire life my mother ever reading from the Bible or ever praying. My dad, who was a World War II veteran, cursed God virtually every day. I was around him throughout his entire life, right up to his death from cancer in 1976.

Junior high school came, and I played in the intramural football program, which was touch football, not tackle football, because in junior high school, there was not any organized football programs in Wichita at that time. I played basketball and was on the team and as an eighth grader and ninth grader, I started on the basketball team. Junior high school did offer a track program in the spring of the year, and I ran track as they called it back then.

When I went to high school, I was introduced to organized coached football, and I naturally went out for football. I started out as an end, probably because of my height of just over six feet, but I was not a heavy kid and only weighed somewhere around one hundred eighty pounds at that time. I then went from football to basketball, and that was where I excelled. As a sophomore, I played and was probably the seventh or eighth man on the team. From basketball, I went on to play baseball where I probably had more natural talent than any of the other sports, but football became my focus.

After high school, I went on to play football at Wichita State University where, because of my high school career, I was awarded an NCAA scholarship for football. If this did not happen, I probably would not have been able to attend a college or university due to the cost involved, and my family would not have been able to help me much with the cost of school. My college career at WSU lasted three years, and during that time, I was married to a girl I knew from high school, and we started our lives together.

My wife's dad was a salesman for a national television manufacturer, and because of his position in the company, when a manager's position at a new warehouse facility opened, I got the job, and my wife worked with me in that warehouse in Denver, Colorado. I was the manager; she took care of the paperwork, inventory, billing, and all the other duties. I called on the various accounts we had in the

Denver area and would make sure their orders were received when they needed them.

Approximately five or six years later, my wife and I went through a divorce. We had one child who was not quite three years old at the time. After the divorce and all the ramifications of that type of event in a person's life, I went out into the world; and I started, after a short time, dating again, which I found rather difficult because of the time frame, six or seven years, since I had been on a date; and it was hard to remember how the dating protocol went; and it had obviously changed since I was in college.

I later was questioned by one of my customers if I had started seeing anyone since my divorce, to which I responded that I had been out a few times but nothing of any real meaning or potential outcome. I was asked if I had ever thought about dating Sally Armstrong. Her husband had been one of my customers and had been killed in a racing accident about one year prior, and I am not real sure what my initial response was, but nothing happened immediately.

As I traveled my territory for a national spark plug manufacturer, a couple of the customers I called on brought up Sally's name to me as someone I should consider dating because she would be "a lot of fun." After having more than one person bring up Sally to me, I decided that when I returned to Wichita, I would give her a call, which I did. I went by her business, which was her former husband's prior to his death, and I found her there, washing her car. I asked if she would like to go to Doc's Restaurant for a glass of tea; she accepted my meager offer.

When we arrived at Doc's, since it was in the middle of the afternoon, the restaurant was almost completely vacant of people eating. We were seated in a small booth, and we ordered our iced tea. The conversation was very casual, nothing being said about the death of her husband and nothing about my divorce; we just sat there and talked about mutual friends. I remember the day, and I was wearing dark-green slacks and a white-and-green print shirt, white belt, and white shoes. Remember, this was the seventies, and I had basically just finished my day of calling on accounts, so we were casual. Sally was wearing a pair of blue jeans and a light blue top with black flats.

When the iced tea was brought to our booth and placed on the table, the waitress asked if we needed anything, and I replied, "no, just some time." Sally went to reach and get the sugar, and she knocked over her glass of iced tea, and it headed right for me. I jumped out of the booth and escaped being soaked with her glass of iced tea. I later told everyone she did that on purpose to try and soak my green slacks.

All the people who had told me I needed to date Sally were all correct in the statements about how much fun she would be, but she was also a consummate lady. We continued to date for a while, and each time, it seemed something happened that just made me grow closer to her. At this time, a permanent relationship and marriage was totally out of my thought process, but Sally was some great person!

Ultimately, I asked her to marry me, and she accepted my proposal, and we were married a short time later and started our lives together. This was in 1974, and it has been a long and prosperous, both financially and spiritually, journey together. There have been ups and downs that come with all marriages, but we have stayed the course and are looking toward our fiftieth anniversary together.

I told you earlier that I basically had very little to no faith even though from time to time, I would attend a church service of various denominations for many years. Sally, on the other side of this coin, had a deep-rooted faith, and she had been raised in the Episcopal faith, and she always longed to return to that worship style, but Episcopal churches were few and far between it seemed. No matter what was going on, I saw Sally staying true to her beliefs in the Lord and living a life that would honor her beliefs.

I was a totally different story; I knew who God and Jesus were, but I had no relationship with either of them. However, I was not going to try to persuade Sally to my way of thinking, could not even if I had been stupid enough to try, so she continued to be a rock in her belief, and I continued to be in charge of my life. My being in charge of my life did not go badly, but looking back, it sure could have been much better and much stronger had I followed Sally at an earlier time.

My life went south because I was deeply involved with alcohol, and it virtually took over my life. I became what is termed a controlled alcoholic. I functioned well at whatever I was doing to earn a living and, in fact, was very fortunate to excel in the area of managing the parts, service, and body shop areas of new car dealerships. The problem was in so many dealerships, alcohol was a very present danger and was readily available. Management in some dealerships used it on a regular, daily basis. Having a drink or two at lunch was the norm, and I fell right into that crazy lifestyle, and it eventually almost cost me my life.

Sally was always supportive of me and always gently trying to help me to give it up. I do not know the pain she suffered because of my alcoholism, and I will probably never know, but I am sure she did suffer, but to what degree, I will never know. Finally, there came a morning when I got up, Sally was getting ready to go to work, I was so hungover that every part of me was in pain. I went to the bathroom, and I looked into the mirror, not a smart move for an alcoholic, and what I saw was grotesque. I felt like I heard a voice telling me, "I was a better man than that, and I had a future." I grabbed the counter, and I prayed. I prayed to a Lord that I did not have a relationship with, but a Lord that knew me inside and out.

In that prayer, I begged forgiveness, and I asked Jesus to help me. I told Jesus that if He would help me, I would give up alcohol and stop drinking. I know that Jesus knew that I was serious about what I had promised, and because of the pureness of my heart in this matter, Jesus took the alcohol and the desire for it totally away. That was the first day of the rest of my life. Some would say that was my resurrection day, and I was now a different person.

When this took place after offering a prayer of faith, asking the Lord Jesus to help me, I felt, and in some miraculous way, the problem of alcohol lifted from my body and my mind. That very day convinced me concerning the power of prayer and the power of prayer lifted up to Jesus in faith would heal the sick, and believe me, I was sick. After that morning, I was made well, and I started living a different life, a life devoted to the Lord, which ultimately lead to the ministry.

COLON CANCER MIRACULOUSLY REMOVED

Early in the process of coming into the ministry, there was a group of men, which varied from approximately sixteen to as many as thirty, that gathered every Monday morning at eight o'clock for breakfast (we liked to say a man's breakfast). This breakfast, a man's breakfast, was one that a cardiologist would literally tell us we were headed for heart attacks, especially if this breakfast was a normal thing instead of once a week. Some cardiologists might even condemn it for a regular once-a-week happening as too much, but we were in Texas, along the Gulf Coast, so we suffered through the breakfast.

Each week, we would gather; a few of us were the cooks, so we arrived to start cooking at about seven o'clock on Monday mornings. Each cook had their area they prepared, but this breakfast consisted of bacon, sausage, hash brown potatoes, eggs, biscuits, and, of course, gravy, with coffee and juices. All men were invited to this event and men from every church gathered for this weekly breakfast. Donations were accepted to pay for all the food, and we never had a problem receiving enough money to pay for the food. As a matter of fact, we had some extra every week, which was kept and accounted for and used to benefit the community.

The format of this breakfast, besides eating, was after we finished eating and we were all gathered around the table or tables moved together to make one large table, one of the leaders would start off by reading a scripture of his choice and subsequent devotional, which related to the scriptures read. These scriptures usually related to our purpose of gathering and offering intercessory prayers for those in need within our community.

When the reading of scriptures and the devotional were completed, we started around the table, and each person in attendance was given the opportunity to lift up a person or two for us to pray for at the end of the morning, usually around ten o'clock on Monday morning. On this particular morning, two of the men were going to prepare for colonoscopies that very week. The two men in question were John and Jim, who were regular members of this Monday morning breakfast, and each one was lifted up to Jesus in prayer, with the plea that their individual procedure would be successful and that all would be well.

The day came for the colonoscopies, and both men went to the place where their procedure was to take place. Members of the breakfast group went along with each member just for comfort and to give the group a report on the results so we would know what took place with each one of them. The report on John came back without any issues, but the report on Jim was another story. Jim had a rather large growth, a little larger than a normal marble, located right in the ninety-degree bend of the colon. Because of the location and the physical size of this growth, the doctors decided to take a biopsy, a measurement of the growth, and the exact location; and a picture was also taken. The biggest problem with this growth was its location in the ninety-degree bend of the colon, and it was on the outside of the bend.

If they tried to remove the growth, and the doctor perforated the colon, an emergency surgery would need to take place to repair the perforation so infection would not be transferred into the lower intestinal area of the lower stomach. Jim and everyone were told of what they had found, and they were also told that the biopsy would be sent off to the lab for analysis to determine if it was a cancerous growth, which would take approximately two to three days.

The tests were done on the sample, and the results came back that the growth was indeed cancerous and needed to be removed. The arrangements for this surgical procedure and the surgical team were being gathered in case they needed to repair a perforated colon. The men gathered the following Monday for breakfast, and the results of Jim's colonoscopy were given, including the diagnosis of the cancerous growth within his colon. The group gathered after breakfast, placed Jim in a chair, all laid their hands on Jim, and prayer was lifted up to the Lord Jesus according to the scriptures in the book of James chapter 5. At the end of the prayer, Jim was anointed with olive oil, and the Lord was thanked for the healing that would take place.

Later that week, Jim's surgery was scheduled, and the doctor working on the colon told everyone there, including Jim's wife, Maria, what to expect and that he felt like all would go well and he would be back out to talk to us in about one hour. All in attendance took our seats in the waiting area, and everyone settled in with coffee, and I read from James chapter five and reminded everyone that we had gathered around Jim and had prayed for healing and had anointed him with olive oil.

To pass the hour, all of us there read from the Bible and talked about the scripture that had just been read. Time always seems to drag in a situation like this, but when scriptures are read and discussed, it always makes the time go by faster. But in this case, someone noticed that it had been almost two hours since the doctor had left to start the procedure. Doubts started to rise up about Jim's condition, and we started to wonder if something had gone wrong. I spoke up at this time, and I told everyone that we needed to trust the Lord Jesus and the doctors. I told everyone that we did not need to build a bridge to go over a creek until we knew for sure there was a creek.

It seemed like I no more than said that than the doctor walked into the waiting room, and none of us will ever forget the look of dismay and shock on the doctor's face as he started to talk to us about Jim and his growth. The doctor showed us the picture of the growth, the measurements of exactly where this growth was located in the ninety-degree bend of Jim's colon. He also went over the lab report, telling us that this growth was a cancerous growth. Then he dropped the bomb on us. The doctor told us he wanted to show us the current picture of this exact location within Jim's colon and pictures of the entire colon. There was no evidence of the growth anywhere, and this doctor finally told us that he "did not know what could have happened!"

Maria stepped forward, took the doctor's hand in hers, and she told the doctor that everyone here knew exactly what happened, and then she told the doctor of the prayer breakfast group and how they had prayed over Jim. Maria told the doctor that she and all of us gathered believed that the great healer, Jesus, had removed that growth. This doctor had no response, but we all knew what had taken place and we all knew and believed it was because of a group of men who had faith in what they were told in the book of James. They followed God's instruction, and because of faith, Jim's growth had been completely removed.

At this writing, Jim is still alive and well with no further colon issues.

THE HOT ROCK

This is the story of a young lady who was diagnosed with stage 4 ovarian cancer. Right after the diagnosis, she went to MD Anderson Cancer Center in Houston, Texas, for treatment. The treatment plan included chemotherapy, some radiation, and at the end surgery, removing the cancerous tissue. The problem with Sherri's cancer was it had progressed to the final stage, stage 4, which in most every case means the treating hospital has its hands full, with not much positive hope. I give you this information before I tell you about my connection and time spent with an amazing young lady.

I was told about Sherri by a friend of mine who was good friends with her dad. My friend, Wade, told me about this young lady and her cancer, and since I had been fishing with her dad, he wanted me to know and wanted me to contact her through email and start to pray for and with her. I made the contact with Sherri, and we started our connection, which lasted just short of two years.

When Sherri would send me an email, it would normally at first be right after a chemo treatment and she was suffering the side effects of that treatment, and I would write a prayer for her and send it to her via email. When the chemo started, there was good news; the cancer was diminishing, and things looked much better than the staff at MD Anderson thought at first, so our hopes were elevated, and it seemed that Sherri was on the way to recovery and the real possibility of a cancer-free outcome.

Sherri told me, in one of our email conversations, about a trip that she and her husband had always dreamed of, and that was to go to the southwestern part of Montana and see the mountains. During our communication, I told Sherri that I had some friends in Montana, and when she was well, my wife and I would load her and her husband in our motor home, and we would take off, and we would all go to Montana to see the beauty of the Rocky Mountains in the southwestern part of the state. I told Sherri that my wife and I had hunted elk in that part of Montana, and we talked about the high mountain camp where we lived when we were hunting.

After almost one year of chemo and radiation, the time came when surgery was to be performed to remove the remaining part of the tumor and, hopefully, all of the cancerous tissue. On the day of the surgery, it seemed like it took an extremely long time for the surgery to be completed, but in reality, it was just a little over two hours. Those two hours seemed much longer even though I spent my time reading and studying scripture from the Bible.

Finally, the surgeon came to the waiting room, and he gave the family and guests the news that he and the team felt real good about the way the surgery went and that he felt like there would be a positive outcome. About one week later, a scan was performed at the hospital, and there was no indication of any cancerous cells present at that time. Remember, this all took place over twenty-seven years ago, so the testing and the technology were not what it is today, but everyone was uplifted, and we were told that the hospital would look again in thirty days.

During those thirty days, Sherri went through the healing process of getting over the major surgery she had endured. The time came, and the date was set for the next scan to be done, but for all that Sherri told the doctors, there was a very optimistic mood, and the feeling was the scan would come back clean. The scan was completed on the day it was scheduled for, and then the only thing that had to be done was to wait two days for the results of the scan, but Sherri and her family were filled with optimism.

Sherri and her family returned to the hospital for the consultation with the doctors and what the plan for the future would be. When a person goes for this type of meeting, there is always some doubt and fear. I believe that is normal, and I know when I go through one of these consultations after a test, I always have some doubts. I do not know, and I cannot say that was totally true of Sherri because she was an eternal optimist. The group went into the consultation room, and the doctors came in and sat down with their reports from the scan of a couple days prior. The doctors opened up their report, and they gave the family a copy for them to read and follow along as the report was given.

I said that hopes were high, and the family was full of optimism, but the doctors did not have good news. The scan had detected some active cancer cells, and they needed to do another test and retrieve some of these cells to verify that they were the same type of cancer. If they were the same cancer, then a treatment program would be discussed at that time. Sherri sent me an email with the news, and even though I responded in a positive manner, I sat there in front of my computer and cried. This was not what I wanted to hear, and I could tell by Sherri's email the news was not what she wanted either.

So the test was scheduled, and some of the cancer cells were retrieved, and the diagnosis of those cells being the same cancer was confirmed. That news was bad enough, but the treatment process going forward was termed as the last hope. The doctors were recommending a treatment that had been successful, but everyone needed to know it was experimental. They were recommending a stem cell transplant procedure. The doctors would harvest stem cells from Sherri's bone marrow, and they would verify they were pure cells, no cancer, then they would grow those cells and then replant the good stem cells back into Sherri.

This process leading up to the implantation of the harvested stem cells would be just about one month away. The process was started immediately, and the stem cells were taken from Sherri's bone marrow, and the growing of the cells began. The preliminary processes were completed, and the day came for the doctors to implant these stem cells back into Sherri and let them attack the cancer cells and destroy the cancer. After this procedure was over, Sherri was told that there was nothing that could be done, and the hope was, she would remain pain-free in her lower abdomen for ninety days.

Sherri decided that she would come to her dad's beach cabin and spend some time there alone, just walking on the beach and being in communion with her Lord. When she arrived at her dad's beach cabin, she discovered she had left the keys to the cabin hanging on the hook back at her home in the Conroe area. She contacted me to see if I could open a storage room door below her dad's cabin because there were spare keys hidden in that room. I responded and went to her dad's cabin and was able, without much trouble, to open the door, and she retrieved the spare keys.

Sherri and I spent some time talking and praying before I left, and I told her that if she needed me for anything to please call me, and I would do whatever she needed me to do. I was going to preach at a Sunday evening service at a local church, so I invited Sherri to come to the service. She told me that her dad and mom were on their way to the beach, and she would bring them with her. To say the least, I was really excited, and the message for that Sunday evening service was "Keeping the Main Thing the Main Thing."

Sherri and her parents came to the service, and after the service, Sherri told me that she really needed to hear that message about keeping Jesus the main thing in our lives. I never understand how our Lord can bring us just what we need just at the exact time we seem to need it. This has happened many times over the years, where people have told me they really needed to hear what was said in the message delivered that day.

Thirty days after the implantation of the stem cells, all was well, and Sherri decided it was time for her to return to her home and get back to attending her church and being a part of her Sunday school class again. Even though we did not have many conversations or meetings while Sherri was at the beach, those conversations we had were enough, and I felt like the procedure was a success.

Sixty days into the recovery and sixty days after the stem cells were implanted, Sherri contacted me and wanted to make sure that my wife and I could head to Montana right after she was given the clean bill of health and was pronounced cancer-free. The date was set, and we started to make the preparations for the trip, and the excitement started to grow because I think I wanted to see the mountains of southwestern Montana as much as Sherri said she did.

About fifteen days after this conversation and the setting of the date for the trip to Montana, Sherri went back to the hospital because she had felt some pain in her lower abdomen. When she arrived at the hospital, they ran the test to see if the cancer was back or if it was something else causing the pain. The results showed that the cancer was back, and it had spread throughout her body. The doctors told her that they had nothing else they could do because the stem cell process was their last hope.

When Sherri told me of this, I got on the phone, and I called a friend of mine who lived in Helena, Montana. When I got him on the phone, I told him about Sherri, and I told him I needed a favor, to which he responded he would do anything he could do. I asked him to get me some dirt from Montana. When I said that, he interrupted me and told me that it was January in Montana; there was over one foot of snow on the ground, and the ground was frozen. I asked if he had any dirt in a flowerpot that he was not using, and he said he did not think of that. I asked for some pictures of the stars from the high mountain camp, no problem, and finally I asked for a flat rock, again no problem. He told me he would put this stuff in the mail the next day.

A few days later, I received a package from my friend in Helena, Montana, and when I opened it up, I found a small zip lock bag with dirt in it, three pictures of the stars in the sky from the high mountain camp, and a flat rock about four inches by five inches, perfect. I received a call from my friend Wade, and he told me Sherri's dad had called him and that Sherri was in the hands of hospice due to the cancer going wild throughout her body. Wade told me that Sherri had told her dad that she wanted to see me at her home in the Conroe area. I agreed to come and see her. When Wade found out, he asked if he could ride with me so he could see Sherri's dad.

Wade and I loaded up in my pickup, and we headed to Jim's home in the Cut and Shoot area, just outside of Conroe, Texas, which would be about a two-hour drive from the beach. We talked about Sherri, and then we really talked about her dad and where he was with what had happened and the fact that he had questioned why God would let this happen to someone like Sherri. I told Wade that I did not know the answer to that question, and I believed there was no answer, and we left it at that, but I knew Jim would ask me about this question at a later date.

Jim, Wade, and I went out to lunch together, and then I followed Jim to Sherri's home. This day, early in February, was not a cold day, but the temperature when we arrived at Sherri's home was in the upper forties, so it was not a hot or even warm day. I had my box of stuff from Montana in the truck on the floor in the backseat area. When I got out of the truck, I grabbed the box, and we headed inside to see Sherri.

There were three of Sherri's girlfriends there, visiting her, and the hospice people were also there, administrating medications to Sherri. The hospice people left and told Sherri they would see her in about three hours, and they left. Wade just spoke to Sherri, and then he and her dad, Jim, left and went to another part of the house, leaving me with Sherri and her three girlfriends. I told Sherri I would not stay long and when I said that she told me we had some things to discuss before I could leave. That was the way Sherri was; she was always thinking about getting things in order.

Sherri then asked about the box I was carrying, and I told her I had some things for her from Montana. I opened the box, and I took out the bag of dirt and told her this was dirt from southwest Montana, and she took the bag, smiled, and passed it on to her friends. These three girlfriends looked a little puzzled that I would bring Sherri a bag of dirt from Montana, but then they did not know our story and deal about Montana.

The next thing in the box was the pictures of the stars in the sky taken at about seven thousand five hundred feet up in the mountains. The sky is so big and dark it makes the stars seem to be much larger and brighter than the ones we see in Texas. Next, I took out the rock. It was wrapped in a paper towel, I told Sherri where the rock came from, and then I took the paper towel off the stone, and that was when I felt something that, at first, did not make sense, but then I realized what was happening.

When I handed the rock to Sherri, she looked at me and asked where the rock had been? I told her in the back seat of my truck. Sherri asked what the temperature outside was, and I told her in the upper forties. Sherri smiled and handed the rock, which was real hot to the touch, to her friends; all of them remarked about the hot rock.

At this they all excused themselves and left, leaving Sherri and me alone in her room.

Sherri and I discussed the heat we felt from the rock, and we both knew it was a sign from our Lord, letting us know that He was there with us. Our conversation covered many things for the next few hours, but two things stood out. Sherri wanted me to confirm that I would spend my life serving our Lord and that I would work to bring her dad to a relationship with Jesus before it was too late. I left Sherri when the hospice people came back. We shared a prayer together, thanking our Lord for always being with us and for making us aware of His presence that day.

Wade and I left and headed back to the beach, and I told him about the hot rock incident, and he just laughed. I also said a private prayer, asking my Lord to give me a sign when He came to receive Sherri into His arms to take her to her eternal home. It was sixteen days later, and I was working on a man's boat dock. It was a very warm day with bright sunshine and virtually no wind. At just a few minutes after one o'clock, I felt like I was placed inside of a freezer; the cold was evident, and it totally surrounded me. I told my coworker we needed to stop and pray because Jesus had just taken Sherri to the Father's mansion.

That evening, I received a call from Jim, Sherri's dad, and he told me that at about ten minutes after one, Sherri left this world. He also told me he needed to talk to me about this rock from Montana. I agreed to meet with him on Friday and that we could meet at his beach house and talk. Jim called me Friday at about one thirty, and I went over to his beach house, expecting to be asked some very tough questions about Sherri, her death, and why God allowed this to happen.

When I arrived at Jim's, I went into the door, and he was standing there waiting on me. We hugged each other, and he invited me inside and told me to have a seat. Jim sat down in a chair right directly across from me, and he looked at me and said, "Tell me about this hot rock deal and tell me what that was all about." I explained the rock, the pictures, and the dirt to Jim, and then I told him that when I took the rock out of the box, removed the paper towel, the rock felt really hot, and Sherri and her friends all felt the same thing. I told Jim that Sherri and I knew it was a sign from our Lord, letting us know he was there with us. Jim told me that was exactly what Sherri told him.

I was waiting on Jim to ask me why this happened, but instead, he asked me if I could help him with his salvation so that he could be with Sherri. I told Jim I would walk him through the scriptures found in Romans, but it was up to him to accept the free gift of salvation from our Lord Jesus, the Christ. The true miracle was that Jim accepted the Lord as his Savior that day. The celebration of life for Sherri was the next day, Saturday, and Jim told me that Sherri had wanted me to put the Montana dirt on her casket as it was lowered into the grave, to place the pictures in the coffin with her, and she had given Jim the hot rock, which Jim said was still hot when Sherri gave it to him.

About ten days later, Jim was diagnosed with a cancerous brain tumor that could not be removed. Jim left this world to be with his daughter less than three months after Sherri left. I can only imagine how that reunion went in heaven. Because of a hot rock, a man who had never had a relationship with the Lord received the Lord of lords as his Lord and Savior, assuring Jim his salvation and his eternal life.

DESTROYED LIVER

Back almost thirty years ago, when I was serving a small church in Northeast Texas, one of the leaders of the church, Bud, came to me on a Tuesday, as I remember, at the church office. For Bud to come to the church during the week was not something uncommon, and the times we spent together reading, discussing scripture, discussing church opportunities, and basically spending time together in the Lord's house in holy discussions were precious memories. On this particular Tuesday, Bud came to talk about a lady he knew who lived in the area and had lived in the area most of her life.

At that time, I was holding a Wednesday evening prayer service where part of the congregation would come and I would deliver a short message, backed up with scripture, concerning prayer and the power of prayer. These services on Wednesday evenings were more about praying for others in the community than it was about a structured worship service even though the Lord was praised throughout the service. One of the things I truly believe is that we really have no power in and of ourselves, but when we turn our petitions and wants over to the Lord, then we are counting on Him and His power, which is granted to us because of our belief in Jesus, but He is the one with the power. We are just instruments through which His power will flow.

Bud sat down in my office, and he began to tell about a lady named Pat. Pat, as much as Bud knew, had no church home, but he believed that she did have a relationship with the Lord. Bud was not sure how strong this belief was, but he did believe that she did have a belief in the Lord Jesus. Bud told me that Pat had been fighting liver cancer for a couple of years he knew of but was unsure of the total length of time she had been fighting this cancer of her liver.

One of the things Bud told me about Pat was that she had been traveling to Houston to MD Anderson Cancer Hospital during this whole time and had been through several types of treatment including chemotherapy, radiation, and transplant surgery, all to no real avail. She would get to the point, with the treatment, where she could feel like she would be deemed cancer-free only to have one setback after another.

She was at the point with her treatment where MD Anderson had told her there was nothing left they could do for her. She was told they had no more experimental treatment options because they had exhausted all of those options. Pat was given a disc that contained many images of the progression, remission, recurrence, progression, remission, and on and on to this point where they had nothing to offer her. They gave her a copy of this disc, and she told them she was going to try the cancer center in Little Rock, Arkansas, to see if they had something for her in the form of a new treatment.

Pat had run into Bud at one of the local restaurants, and they talked about her cancer and where she was in her treatment. This is what Bud wanted to talk to me about that Tuesday in my office. Bud asked me if I felt like if we gathered around Pat at the Wednesday evening service, laid hands on her, prayed the scriptures found in James chapter 5, and anointed her with oil, that would help. I asked Bud if what he truly wanted was to do a service of healing for Pat, and he replied yes, if I was willing to do that for her.

Arrangements were made for Pat to come to my office at the church. Bud agreed to go get her and bring her there for a consultation, and she came later that Tuesday afternoon. We talked about her condition, and I could tell that she was scared about the prognosis, but she had not given up hope. Pat had several questions concerning what this healing prayer service was going to be about, and she really wanted to know what it would do for her.

During our conference, I asked Pat to tell me about her faith and what she believed, and I told her to emphasize her belief in what Jesus could do for her. Pat told me that she had been raised in a church and that her mother, including her father when he was not working, would take her to church most Sundays while she was growing up. She told me that when she went away to attend college, she wondered away from church and basically did not attend any church services while she was at school, but when she would come home to visit, her parents always took her with them to church on Sunday.

Pat also told me that when she graduated from college and she met her husband-to-be, neither one of them went to church on a regular basis, but he had been raised by his parents pretty much the same way she remembered her childhood up to and through becoming a young lady. At this point, I questioned her knowledge of scripture and I found that Pat had a pretty good basic knowledge of scripture, and she was a person who prayed to Jesus. I felt really good about our time together that Tuesday afternoon, so the service for her was set for the following Wednesday evening at seven o'clock.

Wednesday came, and Pat and her husband, Bob, came together, and they took a seat about in the middle of the sanctuary. We started the service with a hymn and then a short message. After that, I told the members in attendance a little bit about Pat and a little bit about her condition. I told them we were going to place Pat in a chair, which was already positioned at the front of the sanctuary in the center, we were going to gather around her, lay hands on her, pray the scriptures from James chapter 5, and anoint her with oil.

Pat took her place in the chair, and all the believers gathered around her, laid their hands on her, and I prayed the scriptures found in James chapter 5, asking our Lord Jesus to heal her completely, and then I anointed her with oil. I had a very distinct feeling come over me at the end of this, and I looked at Pat and told her I felt like she was healed. I have had this feeling before, but I had never had this feeling since that Wednesday evening following the laying on of hands, prayer for healing, and anointing with oil.

The next day, Pat and Bob headed for her appointment with the doctors at the cancer hospital in Little Rock, Arkansas. Pat had told me she was not exactly sure what was going to happen in Little Rock, but she was pretty sure they would review the disc, then run a scan of her liver and possibly the rest of her body, do some blood tests, and then possibly meet with their decision concerning any treatment options the next day, on Friday. I asked Pat to call me as soon as she had any information, no matter what that information happened to be.

Friday came, and I was looking forward to hearing from Pat and what was going to happen concerning her liver cancer. Friday was normally my day off, and I usually played golf on that day with a group of men, and this Friday was no different. We all arrived at the golf course, warmed up a little on the driving range, and we were off to play the eighteen holes and hopefully finish around noon so we could all get a bit to eat and talk about the round of golf we had played.

Friday went by in what was a normal fashion, and I basically forgot about Pat and Bob. Since I did not hear from them, Saturday came and went just like normal, with me playing another round of golf but with different people at a different course. Saturday golf was normally a couples' thing with my wife and I joining with another couple, normally another pastor and his wife, to play a round of golf and enjoy the day. We started off on the first tee like normal, with me saying a short prayer asking the Lord to bless us as we played and to allow us to bless Him while we played.

After our round of golf, the four of us went to a local restaurant, and we enjoyed the meal together, and I think that my wife and I had outplayed the other couple, so they were the ones blessed with the opportunity to pay for our dinner together. When we left and headed home, I thought about Pat and Bob, checked my phone for a message, but there was nothing there that gave me some thoughts of concern, but I needed to prepare for Sunday and the worship service that would take the rest of the day and into the early evening.

Sunday came, and the worship service went well, and the Lord was praised, and I believe He was blessed with what we had done, and it seemed like many were blessed by what was said in the sermon. My wife and I were invited to go with Bud and his wife, Lois, out to eat after the service, and we headed to a local Mexican food restaurant we all enjoyed. During the meal, Bud inquired about Pat and if I had heard anything from her. I told him that I had not heard anything but that Monday I would call her cell phone and see if I could get any information concerning her treatment.

Monday came, and when I arrived at the church and my office, I sat down and called Pat's cell phone to try and get some information concerning any results she had received, but her cell phone went right to voice mail, so I left her a message to call me and let me know what the progress was and what she had found out concerning treatment options. Bud called me and told me that Pat and Bob were not at their home because he had gone by to check, and he felt like they had been gone because of the papers on the porch and mail in the mailbox. This would indicate they were still in Little Rock.

I was busy the rest of the day with hospital visits and a couple of meetings, so Monday came and went with no response from Pat or Bob, leaving me without any information concerning her diagnosis. Tuesday came and went with no contact from Pat or her husband Bob. Wednesday came, and I prepared for the prayer service scheduled to take place that evening at seven o'clock.

I arrived at the church for the Wednesday evening prayer service about half an hour before the service was to start, and I made sure everything in the sanctuary was ready for the impending service. The people started to arrive, and it appeared that we would have a few more in attendance than we normally would have for this service. At the appointed time, I started the service with the singing of a hymn and an opening prayer.

At this time, I would normally start reading from Scripture and delivering a short devotional prior to the start of lifting prayers up to our Lord Jesus. I heard the doors to the sanctuary open and when I looked to the back of the sanctuary, I saw Pat and her husband, Bob, walking into the sanctuary. Pat continued to the front and Bob took a seat about midway in the sanctuary. Pat asked me if she could speak to the members in attendance, and I gave her permission to do so.

Pat started off by thanking me and the members for what they had done for her just one week prior, and she told us that she could not put in words how grateful she was for our action of laying on of hands, prayer, and anointing of her with oil. She told us that when they arrived at the hospital in Little Rock and sat down with the doctors, she gave them the disc from MD Anderson, and when they viewed it, they told them they needed to run a scan on her liver to have a comparison to compare with the disc.

The scan was already scheduled, and Pat told us they said they would be able to meet with her and give her the results in approximately two hours. The scan was performed, and Pat said they waited. About an hour after the scan was completed, the doctor came and told her they would like to run another scan and that they were ready to do that immediately. No information was given to Pat or Bob, but she went for the second scan.

After the completion of the second scan, she and her husband returned to the waiting area to wait to hear from the doctors concerning the results of the two scans. In about one hour, the doctor came in and told her that they wanted to do a full body scan to see where there might be further cancer that had migrated from the liver. The doctor told Pat the full body scan was scheduled for four o'clock that afternoon, and if they wanted to get something to eat, this would be a good time.

Pat said they went to the cafeteria to eat, but she just did not want to eat anything because she was becoming fearful of what they were finding. Bob did his best to try and get Pat to relax and wait for all the results, which was easier said than done. They returned at the appointed time, and the scan proceeded. When the scan was completed and Pat was dressed, they were told that there would be a meeting with the doctors in the morning at ten o'clock, so they went and found a room for the night.

The next day, they arrived for the meeting with the doctors, and they were told there was one more group of tests they needed to perform, and they were set to start shortly. After about two hours of testing, they were told the doctors would meet with them on Monday, but when Monday came, the meeting was postponed until Tuesday right after lunch.

Pat told us that when they arrived for the meeting on Tuesday afternoon, they were taken into a consultation room, and they were just there a few minutes when the door opened and in walked four doctors. They started by showing the disc that Pat had brought with her and reviewing the extent of the cancer that had virtually consumed her liver. Then they put up their disc from the first scan; it was clear. They put up the disc from their second scan, and it, too, was clear. Then they put up the results of the body scan, and it was clear. They reviewed the blood work, and they could not find any cancer cells anywhere.

The doctors wanted to know what happened since she had had the scan done with the results showing her liver consumed with cancer. She told them the story of the prayer service, and the doctors then told her that as far as they could determine, even though they did not understand what had happened, she was completely cancer-free.

Pat told us that she did not totally understand, but she did believe that for some reason, what that reason was she did not know or understand, the prayer that was lifted up to our Lord Jesus reached Him, and she was healed. She made comment to me that she remembered that after the prayer and anointing of her, I had told her I felt she was healed, and through the grace of our Lord Jesus, she was completely healed.

THE SMOKER

One day, I was leaving the hospital in Atlanta, Texas, where I was head of Pastoral Care Services, and a lady stopped me in the hallway. She asked if I was the chaplain, and then she told me her name. Mary told me that her dad was in a certain room and that he was dying from lung cancer and he had turned against God. She asked me if I would go in his room and talk to him about God. I asked her if she knew if her dad had ever accepted Jesus as his Lord and Savior, and she told me she did not think he ever did.

When I started into Robert's room, there was a sign on the door warning of oxygen in use within the room, so no smoking or open flames. I did not have to worry about either, but when I entered, I noticed a pack of cigarettes laying on Robert's portable tray. He looked up at me, and he told me, "I guess you are one of those preachers, and I suppose my daughter Mary sent you in to save me."

I told him who I was and that I was a preacher, but that I was not in his room to preach to him, but rather, I was there at the request of his daughter because she was deeply concerned about him and his illness and his relationship with the Lord. Robert looked at me, and he told me he wanted to ask me a direct question. I told him that would be fine, and he asked "if God is a God of love, why would He cause him to have cancer and would cause him to suffer this way and would probably cause his death because of this lung cancer?"

I told him that I truly wanted to answer his question, but I needed some information from him, so I asked if I could ask him a couple of questions, and he said, "that would be okay." I picked up the pack of cigarettes, and I asked Robert how long he had been smoking. He told me he had started during World War II and had smoked ever since. I said, "So you have smoked at least fifty years?"

He said that would be about right. I asked him if he was forced to start smoking, or if he started voluntarily. He told me that "no one forced him to smoke. He started on his own, and everyone did it."

I took the pack of cigarettes, and I looked at the package, and I found the warning from the surgeon general that smoking may cause cancer. I pointed that out to him, and I asked if he had ever paid any attention to that warning on the side of the package. He told me he had read it but did not pay any attention to what it said. "So Robert, you were able to make the decision to smoke these cigarettes of your own free will," I said. His response was a quiet yes, and then he wanted to know when I was going to answer his questions about God.

I told him that our God was an allowing God and that He loved us so much that He allowed His only son to pay the price of death for our sins so that we could have the chance at eternal life. I also told him about how God gives us free will to make decisions, but that sometimes, we make the wrong decisions, and in some instances, we actually decide to go against a command of God. I related this to the happenings with Adam and Eve in the Garden of Eden when they were confronted by the serpent or the devil. They had complete freedom of will to make their decision concerning the forbidden fruit, but they chose to go against the command of God and eat that fruit.

They committed a sin that has caused mankind a problem ever since, but God even demonstrated His love for them after they had sinned by making them clothes out of the skins of animals. They were rejected from the Garden of Eden, but God continued to love them just the same way He loves us even when we make bad decisions that wind up causing us pain and, in some cases, causing us to lose our lives.

At this point, I shut up and just stood there looking at Robert. I could tell by his facial expression that he was thinking about what I had said and possibly even thinking about his decision to smoke all those years. It seemed like we were quiet for an extremely long time, and then Robert spoke, and he said he had one more question for me. He said, "Why didn't God stop me when I first started to smoke?" I looked at him, and I told him in as soft a voice as I could,

"If God had stopped you then, you would not have had free will to make your decisions in your life, including the decision you made to smoke."

At that time, Robert looked at me, and he wondered if it was too late for him to do whatever it took to get into heaven. I opened my Bible up to the book of Romans and turned to chapter 10, and I walked Robert down what is called the Roman road to salvation. Robert said a prayer, asking his Lord to forgive him of his many sins and to please come into his life and lead him through the rest of his time on earth. I told Robert that it was not too late to quit smoking, and he told me to take the cigarettes with me.

I asked Robert to be sure and tell his daughter that I came to see him and to please tell her what happened and tell her I have your cigarettes. Every day after that, I would make sure to stop by Robert's room and talk with him and to always pray with him and for him before I left his room. It was a couple of weeks later that I received a call from Mary, and she told me that after that day she stopped me in the hallway of the hospital and asked me to visit her dad, he was a totally different person right up to the day he left this world for the eternal world. Mary also told me that he never smoked again after that day.

Robert received peace, and he was made well that day in the hospital because he accepted his responsibility for probably causing the lung cancer that ultimately caused him to lose his life. I will always remember Mary and her dad, Robert, and it was almost one year later while I was looking for something in my desk that I found Robert's pack of cigarettes. You see, my Lord has a way of reminding us of the interactions He has with people we serve as preachers or chaplains.

GOODPASTURE DISEASE

As I remember, it was during the middle of the week, and I had traveled to a small town in Northeast Texas for a monthly meeting with a small group of pastors. This small group, five in total, would meet once a month mid-week at around ten o'clock in the morning, and we would discuss our previous month, if our goals had been achieved, if our ministries were on track for the kingdom of God, and if we were taking care of ourselves both physically and spiritually. This meeting was an accountability meeting between the five of us to help keep each other on track and to help in any way we could if our help was needed.

When we arrived and had our short time of greeting and small chitchat, the very next thing would be for the host pastor to have every one of us take out our cell phones and put them on silent. This was so we could conduct our meeting without the constant interruption of cell phones ringing, beeping, or going off with some exotic ringtone. This gathering was to last until noon, and at that time, we would normally adjourn and go somewhere to eat lunch together. At one of the churches, the ladies of that church always fixed a great meal for us and brought it to us and served it to us at noon, but this was not that church.

Usually after about one hour, we would stop and take a small necessary break, and then after just a few minutes, we would resume. Sometimes, some of the pastors would check their phones and listen to any messages or return a call they thought might need to be answered. Most of us just looked and went back so we could be finished by noon so we could go eat. Food became the priority after almost a two-hour meeting.

My cell phone started buzzing about ten or fifteen minutes before we were to end our meeting, and it had been decided that, due to some minor church things, everyone would be on their own for lunch. My phone would buzz, then it would stop, and I assumed it was going to voice mail, then it would buzz again, and I would assume it was going to voice mail, then it would buzz again, so I felt like there was an emergency of some kind that needed my attention. The meeting came to an end at just the right time, so I checked my phone, and I had six calls from the same number, but it was a number I did not recognize and was not in my huge lists of contacts.

Before leaving the church, I had a good signal, and I returned the call after listening to the voice mails, which just told me to please call. When I called, a man answered, and I asked who it was. He told me it was Larry, whom I knew but was not part of my church, but we worked out at the same gym at the same time in the mornings, so I knew who it was. Larry told me that he was at one of the hospitals in Texarkana, Texas, and that his granddaughter was there, and she was not expected to live. I asked Larry if he had contacted the pastor of his church, and he told me he had but that his pastor would not come because his granddaughter was not a part of that church's membership.

Larry went on to tell me that he needed me to come and pray for her and ask for healing. I asked him a few questions, then I told him it would take me about thirty minutes to get there but that I was on my way. One of the members of the accountability group noticed that I was concerned after getting off the phone, and he asked if everything was all right. I told him briefly about the situation with Larry's granddaughter, and he asked if he could come because he had heard of what had happened with this type of prayer. I told him to come on and witness what would happen.

I traveled with Reverend Mitchell following me to the hospital in Texarkana, and when we arrived, we both retrieved our pastor and chaplain credentials, hung them around our necks, and proceeded to enter the hospital. Once inside, we went to the fourth floor, the medical ICU floor, went to the waiting room where we found Larry, his wife, his son-in-law, and the pastor of the granddaughter's church. Introductions were made, and I suggested we go into one of the available Chaplain Consultation Rooms. We found one that was open, and we entered and began our discussion.

First off, I spoke to Pastor Al, the pastor of Linda's church, Larry's granddaughter, and we discussed what had transpired with Linda to get her to this point. During this discussion, we were told that Linda was pregnant and in her fifth or early sixth month of the pregnancy. I inquired to try and find out if they had any information concerning the unborn baby's condition. I was told they did not know anything about the baby's condition because everything was focused on saving Linda's life.

When I talked to the people who were in this consultation room and told them what I was going to do, Pastor Al, Linda's pastor, excused himself and left the room. I reviewed what I was going to do, and I asked everyone there—Larry, the grandpa, Jim, the son-in-law, and Reverend Mitchell—if they believed that Jesus could heal Linda and make her well. By the statement "make her well," I meant that she would be healed both physically and spiritually, making her whole.

When we left the room, everyone went to the waiting room to wait for me to get this prayer for healing set up in the medical ICU. I spotted Pastor Al, and I asked him to step outside the waiting room with me for a moment. I did this so I could find out where he stood on this healing prayer and why he left the room. He told me that he was not going to be a part of this because when it did not work, he did not want to deal with the aftermath of questions about prayer and prayers that were not answered to the family. I felt like I learned an awful lot about this Pastor Al from his answers to my questions concerning healing prayer.

I went to the nurse's station and talked to the nurse in charge, Pat, and she told me there would be no problem with all of us going into the ICU room and praying for Linda. Then she asked me something I was not expecting. Pat asked if she could be a part of this healing prayer because she had heard of this but never been a part of this type of prayer. I told her she was welcome. On my way back to the waiting room to retrieve everyone, I went into a small room, closed the door, and prayed to my Lord, asking him to be present and to guide my words and to give Linda complete healing.

I retrieved everyone from the waiting room, and we proceeded to Linda's room, picking up Pat at the ICU nurse's station, then we went into Linda's room. We gathered around her, laid our hands on her, prayed the scriptures from James chapter 5, and I anointed her with oil. When we left, Larry thanked me and asked me if I thought our prayer and the laying on of hands worked. I told him that Linda's life was totally in the hands of her Lord Jesus, and we would know soon, very soon.

The next day, a young new resident was going through the Medical ICU, and he looked at Linda's chart. I do not know what he keyed in on, but he inquired of the nurses if she had been checked for Goodpasture disease. The response was no, and he started the test for this disease, which no one there had ever heard of before this day. The test was positive, and he contacted the Mayo Clinic concerning treatment. The people at Mayo asked about Linda's liver function and told the resident that it must be at a certain level or above for her to receive the treatment. The liver function test was performed, and she was indeed able to receive the treatment, so Mayo overnighted the treatment medicines to the hospital in Texarkana.

The next day, the treatment process started and within just a few hours, Linda started to respond in a positive way, so the remainder of the treatment was given to her. Within forty-eight hours, Linda was awake, and she was eating, talking, and actually laughing, and also wanting to know when she could go home. That day, she was placed in a regular room, then came some bad news. The baby she was carrying had not survived this ordeal and needed to be removed from Linda's womb.

Larry contacted me the day Linda was moved to a regular room, and he wanted me to come to Texarkana and visit his granddaughter, so arrangements were made, and I went to the hospital in Texarkana. When I went into Linda's room, she was fully dressed and up and walking around; she was much different now than how she was the last time I saw her. She came and gave me a hug, and I told her at that time I was sorry about the loss of her baby but that I wanted us to pray. We joined hands, and we prayed together, and we thanked the Lord Jesus for what He had done for Linda and her family.

A few months later, I received a call from Linda, and she told me that she was pregnant again, and she was looking forward to the birth of this new baby. I later found out the new baby was born without any complications, so Linda and her husband were proud parents of a little baby boy.

RACIAL HEALING

Early in my ministry, I was serving a small church in Northeast Texas close to the Arkansas and Louisiana state lines. In this small town, there happened to be another church of the same denomination that was African American. I knew several members of the congregation from serving in a local hospital as a chaplain. This little church had a pastor who was filling the pulpit until the district superintendent found a pastor for this small church, with a congregation of fifteen to twenty attending the weekly Sunday worship service. This church had been through a couple of interim pastors, and it was obvious the district superintendent was having a great deal of trouble finding this church a permanent pastor.

Annually, every pastor in our denomination meets with the district superintendent to discuss the church or churches the pastor is serving. One thing that comes up is whether the pastor is happy and feels good about his appointment, and if he wants to be moved to another church. Several things come into play, or did at that time, concerning whether or not a pastor was or would be moved to another church. When I was asked by the district superintendent if I was happy where I was, I told him that I was but that I wanted another appointment.

The look on the district superintendent's face was one of disbelief. He had never had a pastor tell him he was happy and ask for another appointment. He asked me to explain myself, and I told him that I wanted to stay where I was, but I wanted to be appointed to the African American church as their pastor also, but only if the entire congregation would approve of that appointment. This was something that was just not really ever done, where the congregation, especially one this small, would ever get to approve the pastor who was coming to serve them. Normally, it was a meeting of the members with the district superintendent, and the DS would tell them who was coming, period.

This would be something unusual for a pastor like me, a white guy, to ask to be appointed to serve a black church. I did not see any problem, but I also knew that there full well could be some issues due to my race. I remember the first time this church's pastor had invited me to come and preach one Sunday. I went ready, I hoped, to deliver a message the congregation would receive and that the message would speak to them.

After the service, their pastor told me he needed to talk to me for a few minutes before I left to go to my appointed church to handle the worship service there. Reverend John told me that my message was good and had a lot of merit, but there is one problem. Reverend John told me that he could tell I had never preached to a black congregation before. He told me that I was used to the white congregations because when I asked a question in my message, I did not allow the congregation to respond. I just forged on ahead, leaving this congregation confused. Reverend John told me to relax, and he offered a Sunday in the future for me to return, about six weeks in the future, so I could try it again. I accepted.

Reverend John told me to be ready because when I asked a question, they would answer, but they might ask a question in return, and they would expect me to answer their question. The problem I could see was that when I developed a message, I planned for that message to build in a particular direction to a climax. If the return question led to me answering and altering the direction I had planned, what would I do and how would I get back on the original direction?

I developed a message for the appointed Sunday, but two weeks before I was to return and speak, I contacted Reverend John and told him I wanted him to review my message and give me some direction concerning what to expect as questions from the congregation and what he thought they might ask. Reverend John agreed and he took my message, reviewed it, and then I asked him to write in the margins potential questions he could foresee might be asked of me in response to my questions, and he did just that.

The next Sunday came, and I went to the worship with a much larger case of nerves than normal. I had reviewed the potential questions, and I felt like I was ready, but I was still a little unsure of my capability to deliver a message that would speak to this congregation. During the delivery of the message, every time I asked a question of the congregation, I paused and waited for their response. The first time, they were a little slow in responding because they remembered my first attempt at preaching there, so they felt like I would just go on with my delivery, but this time I waited, and I received an answer.

The next question I asked, I paused, and I received an answer, but I also received a question from another member of the congregation. The really cool thing about the question was the fact that it was one of the responses Reverend John had told me in the review might come my way. I answered the question, and then returned to the message and stayed true to the original direction I had intended the message to travel. At the end of the service, several members of the congregation remarked about the message in a positive way.

After the service, Reverend John and I had a few minutes together, and I asked him how he knew what questions might come back at me because every question asked in response to the original question was one, he had said could be possible. Reverend John looked at me and told me that it was just from a lifetime of preaching in the African American or Black church. That Sunday, Reverend John's ability to teach this white boy how to preach taught me more than I ever learned in preaching class at seminary.

A few weeks later, the district superintendent went to this congregation and told them of my request, and he also had to tell them that Reverend John was going back into retirement. He told this congregation to talk it over, and vote to decide on me, and then let him know so he could go forward filling their pulpit. In about a week, the leadership of this congregation contacted the district superintendent and told him they wanted me to be appointed as their pastor.

Things progressed, and both churches were doing well; both churches were showing growth, but the growth and the response with the African American church was something I would have never thought of, but I could still feel something. I was not sure what the feeling was, but I could feel it. There was a couple, an older couple in the congregation, and Charles had cancer and had been fighting it for several years, and I could tell it was getting closer to the end for Charles.

Merriam, Charles' wife, seemed like she never missed the worship services, but Charles would miss when he was hurting too badly from the cancer or from the treatments. It was winter, and I believe it was January, and Northeast Texas had been hit with one of those winter storms that left more ice than snow, so traveling was treacherous at best. Sunday came, and neither Merriam nor Charles was at church. When I inquired, I was told that Charles was in the hospital in Texarkana, not doing well, and Merriam was with him. After I finished with the worship services at both churches, I returned to the parsonage with my wife, and I went into the bedroom, and I started changing clothes.

My wife could tell that something was up because of the clothes I was putting on; they were warm clothes, so she figured out I was going somewhere, but she was not sure where. She asked, and I told her I had to go to Texarkana to see Charles and Merriam even though the highway was icy in most places and not a smart idea to get out in a car and drive on it, but I felt like I had to go. I left with the warning from my wife to be extremely careful and to call her when I arrived at the hospital in Texarkana.

The twenty-plus-mile trip took almost one hour, but I made it to the hospital without incident. But when I got out of the car and walked about thirty feet, I stepped on some more ice and down I went, more embarrassed and luckily not hurt. I stood back up and walked, much slower, to the door of the hospital and went inside. I made it to Charles's room and knocked on the closed door. I heard a female voice tell me to come in. I opened the door, and there was Charles in the bed and Merriam sitting in a chair beside him.

Merriam asked me what in the world I was doing there. I responded by telling her I had to come to see Charles. Charles was so weak that when he spoke, his voice was so soft and quiet I could just barely hear him, if I heard him at all. Normally, when Charles spoke, there was absolutely no problem hearing his booming deep voice, but today was different. Merriam told me she could not hear him, but she was beside him, and that seemed to be enough.

I needed to hear what Charles was saying because I felt like he was asking me something. The only way I could hear him was to almost get into the bed with him and get right next to his face with my ear. Charles asked me to pray for him, and he told me he wanted Merriam to hold his hand. About the time this happened, the door of the room opened and in walked Charles's and Merriam's daughter, Kim.

Kim was a young single mother, probably in her upper twenties or early thirties, with three beautiful children whom Merriam had been bringing with her to church, but Kim had never attended worship. She asked her mother what I was doing, and I told her that Charles, her dad, had asked me to gather everyone and to have a prayer together. Kim looked at me, and I really do not know what I saw, but I felt it was good. Merriam, Kim, and I gathered around Charles, and we prayed for him, and we prayed for ultimate healing. After the prayer, I said goodbye, and I left, heading back to the parsonage some twenty plus miles away.

On my way home, I could not get the look on Kim's face out of my mind. Her face told me something, and I felt like the look was good. I prayed for Charles, Merriam, and Kim all the way home, and even though it took almost one hour, it seemed like it was just a few minutes. I arrived at the parsonage, and I shared what had happened with my wife. She asked if I had eaten anything, and it was then I realized that I had not eaten since breakfast that morning, and I was in fact starving, so my wife fixed me a great ham sandwich with oven-baked French fries. It was worth the wait.

I heard that Charles had been released from the hospital even though the doctors had warned against it due to his condition, which was not good. I visited Charles a couple of times the following week. The ice was gone, so it was not difficult driving the rest of the week. Sunday came, and at the worship service, Merriam came, and to my surprise, Kim was there with her boyfriend and her children, something I had not experienced or expected.

The service went well with lots of responsive questions during the message, but I had come to look forward to those questions because this congregation was making me into a much better preacher. After the service, I was at the door speaking to the congregation as they left, and the last to leave was Merriam, Kim, her boyfriend, and her children. Kim came to me, and she told me that she had a problem with white people, but when she saw what I had done that Sunday in the hospital room with her dad, she said she could no longer have those feelings about white people anymore.

Merriam and Kim and her children and boyfriend, Raymond, became a regular part of the congregation, and she continued to thank me for what I was doing for her dad, and especially what I had done for her. I thought the prayer I prayed that Sunday in Charles's hospital was strictly for Charles, but it turned out that it was for Kim also.

RECEIVING SALVATION

The event in this story is about Mike, a family man with a wife and four children, living in a city of about two hundred twenty-five thousand people. Mike had his own small contractor business where he did painting and sheet rock installations. Most of his work was new construction, but when he did not have any of that type of construction to do, he and his paint crew would paint homes for people.

Mike was successful in what he did, and his wife was a very important part of his business, like most wives in small businesses, and she was the one who did the payroll, paid the bills, and even helped with some of the job bidding. This family was not a family that would be classed as the typical church family. In fact, most of the family did not attend any church on anything that could be considered a form of regularity.

Mike was a man who had enlisted in the military right after the start of World War II. He was the youngest of three brothers, so when they all decided to enlist, Mike had to tell the army that he was two years older than he really was in order to enlist. During the war, Mike served his country well. He was wounded at least twice in combat, and he was awarded the bronze and silver star. I feel that what Mike saw and what he lived through during that war and his time in combat was the determining factor when it came to his church life.

Mike was in his late fifties, and he noticed a lump under his right arm. This lump did not bother him or keep him from working, but it did grow, and it seemed to be growing at a rapid pace. Finally, the growth was about the size of a golf ball, and then it started to be painful, and it hurt when it was touched or when it was put in a position where during work activities pressure was placed on the growth. Mike finally decided to go to the doctor and get this painful lump checked.

He went to the doctor, and his family doctor examined him. He then referred him to a surgeon. The surgeon did his exam and told Mike that he recommended immediate removal of this lump because of where it was located, under his arm in the armpit area. The surgery was scheduled, and the lump was removed. After removal, the surgeon sent the lump to pathology because of the looks of it. The report came back as cancer, so the surgeon took out more tissue and removed the closest lymph gland.

In this small metro area at that time, they were not well equipped to treat cancer, so the surgeon recommended to Mike and his family that Mike go to Houston, Texas, and MD Anderson Cancer Hospital for evaluation and further treatment. The six-hundred-plus-mile trip was made, and Mike and his wife went to their appointment at MD Anderson. In Houston, the doctors at the hospital gathered all the needed information, reviewed the surgeon's report, the pathology reports, and they started a treatment plan that included chemotherapy.

Back in those days, chemotherapy was a new procedure, and they did not have all the medications they have today to make the treatment easier for the patient. Going through this treatment in those days was horrific, and the suffering after the treatment was tremendous, with no relief for the pain except time to get over it, and then it was normally time for the next treatment.

Mike went through this chemotherapy, and after a few months, he was released from MD Anderson to return home with a good prognosis. Mike was to return to Houston in three months for tests so they could monitor him and make sure the cancer was in remission. Three months went by, and Mike and his wife returned to Houston. The tests were performed, and at this time, he was still in remission; he was to return in another three months.

In another three months, Mike and his wife returned to Houston, and the tests were performed, and once again, his cancer was still in remission. He was told by his doctors they would see him in six months, and if he was still in remission, then they would do annual testing. When Mike and his wife left Houston, heading home, their mental states had finally rose to a level they felt like they would make it. When they arrived home, there was a great neighborhood celebration because of this great positive report.

Some time later, about three to four months, Mike started to have really severe headaches, similar to a migraine, but Mike had never been one to suffer from headaches, especially a headache this severe. His doctors at MD Anderson were contacted, and a scan was scheduled at a local hospital, with the results to be sent to Houston. The day came, and the scan was run, and a growth was detected within Mike's brain. A biopsy was performed, and it was confirmed that the cancer had returned and settled within this growth in Mike's brain.

Mike returned to MD Anderson, and his doctors ran some further tests. Mike and his wife were informed that nothing could be done to remove the growth because it was basically inside the brain, and they would have to cut through the brain to get to the growth. They were told that where this growth was located was at the part of Mike's brain where pain is sensed, and that was why the pain from the headaches had disappeared.

Mike's condition deteriorated rapidly, and Mike wound up in bed with the family taking care of him twenty-four hours a day. At this time, a local pastor started to come by on a daily basis to see Mike. Mike always told his wife that he did not want to see the pastor. Even though Mike refused to see the pastor on a daily basis, the local pastor continued to come to their house every day to try and see Mike. This went on for almost two weeks, and one day, the local pastor did not come by to see Mike.

Another day later, Mike told his wife that he figured she needed to get in touch with the local pastor because Mike wanted to see and talk to him. The local pastor was contacted and within hours of Mike's request to see him, the local pastor was there at Mike's bedside. Mike told the pastor that he knew he was going to die. He also told the pastor about how he never believed in God or His Son, Jesus. Mike wanted to know if the pastor could save him, so he could go to heaven.

The pastor told Mike he could help him receive Jesus, but the pastor would not be able to save Mike; only Jesus could do that. The pastor read from chapter 10 of the book of Romans, and he led Mike in a prayer where Mike asked for forgiveness for his sins, asked Jesus to come into his life as his Lord and Savior. When the pastor left Mike's bedroom, he talked with the wife and told her what had happened. The pastor told Mike's wife that he was sure that Mike had received his salvation and would spend his eternal life with Jesus in heaven.

Three days later, Mike left this world and proceeded to the eternal world. I tell those of you reading this because it is never too late to receive Jesus and your salvation so that you can receive the ultimate healing; that healing is eternal life. If you have not received Jesus as your Lord and Savior, do it today because we do not know if we have or we will be granted tomorrow.

RETURN OF LEUKEMIA

Let me try to tell you the story of Kenneth. He was a young boy of about five years of age at the time I met Kenneth, his mother, father, and sister. All were part of the church, and virtually every Sunday, they were part of the worshipping congregation. The whole congregation loved this family because they knew the history of this family, and some of the congregation knew the mother and father before they ever decided to get married and then in a couple of years start their family with the birth of Kenneth.

Shortly after the birth of Kenneth, somewhere between one and two years, something was wrong, so the tests started with Kenneth, and it was determined that he had a form of childhood leukemia. The decision was made to take him to MD Anderson cancer facility and see what was going to happen. The diagnosis was made, and it was confirmed that this little baby did indeed have leukemia, and treatments were laid out, and the journey to cure this child started.

Somewhere about this time, Pam, Kenneth's mother, became pregnant with their second child. This created some mild complications due to the travel back and forth to Houston for Kenneth's treatments and Pam now carrying her second child. But as mothers and fathers do, they figured out how to navigate these turbulent waters and make it through, juggling their schedules so that Kenneth did not miss any treatments. The second child was born, and it was a little girl, and they named her Chris. From all indications, Chris was a healthy girl, and she instantly started growing like the proverbial weed.

After two long years of treatment, Kenneth was able to "ring out" at MD Anderson in Houston, and he was declared to be cancer-free. This was a long-fought battle, and there would be continual visits to the hospital on regular intervals to monitor and to check and make sure that Kenneth stayed cancer-free. When he was able to "ring out," there was a great celebration at the hospital just like there always is when anyone gets the news that their cancer is in remission and the active cells are no longer detectable. What a day that was!

This is about the time that I came to know this family, and they were a very active part of the church, with both the father and the mother assuming active leadership roles within the church body. Virtually every time there happened to be an event at the church outside the regular Sunday worship services, this family of four would be there, and the whole family would be involved. This was one of those families that every preacher would love to have as many families like this in their church as possible and would never believe there could be too many of them.

A couple of years went by, went by very quickly, and Kenneth started having some problems that manifested themselves in his appetite. His overall presence seemed sluggish, and Kenneth was tired all the time. He went back to MD Anderson and to the doctors who had dealt with him before. Tests were performed, and the family was told the news no one wanted to hear—Kenneth's leukemia was back. But this time, it was much worse, and it was very aggressive. Naturally, the entire family was shaken as was the entire church family. The thing about a close church family is that when one suffers, everyone suffers in some way, shape, or form.

The doctors called for a consultation with the family, and they asked if I would come with them to hear the news and to hear where they would go from this point. The doctors came into the consultation room, and they sat in the chairs in the front of the room at the head of the table. With them they brought folders with tests results, and I imagine everything there was to know about Kenneth and his condition.

The lead doctor started by telling us that Kenneth's leukemia had morphed and even though it was basically the same, it was different in the way it attacked the blood, and the strength of this particular leukemia was something they had never seen before. What we were waiting for was the information concerning the type of treatment and if there would be more than one treatment option. The lead doctor finally told us he was going to now finally discuss the treatment plan for Kenneth.

I do not think anyone there, including me, expected to hear what we were about to hear. He told us that they did not have any treatment plans or options for Kenneth. I remember he paused for just a moment, and really, before what he said had a chance to soak into our minds, he said the word *but.* I do not ever remember that word sounding so good to me before, and I know it sounded good to Kenneth's father and mother because of the look on their faces.

We were told that even though MD Anderson had no treatment for this, a cancer hospital in London, England, had a treatment that had been very successful, somewhere in the seventy-five percent success range. Anytime a family deals with cancer, especially cancer in a child, to hear that the treatment that is available has a success rate of seventy-five per cent, well, that is great news. We were also told that this treatment was very aggressive, and it was much more dramatic than Kenneth had ever been through to date. Everyone was assured by the doctors that Kenneth could handle the treatment.

The people of the church were informed, and plans were made to take up special offerings for this family to help with the expenses of traveling to Houston every week for at least five months during the duration of this treatment. I talked to Kenneth's father, and I told him what was going on with the church, and he broke down and cried. He was very scared that he might lose his son, and he did not know what he would do if and when that happened. I told him that we did not know that would happen, and we were told there was a seventy-five percent probability that Kenneth would come through this treatment, and this cancer would be defeated again, hopefully permanently.

I also told him that we had someone on our side that could heal anything without any problem, and we needed to keep our faith and believe that Jesus was on our side. I told him that Jesus would be going through this treatment with us, but especially with Kenneth. When I talked with Kenneth, his faith in Jesus first and then his faith in the doctors second made me feel somewhat inferior to him.

Kenneth told me how thankful he was that Jesus had found this hospital in London, England, with this treatment that would take care of him.

During this long treatment process, Kenneth's situation was well known throughout the entire community, and the people in this little rural community were taking care of everything they could take care of—taking care of the other two children, making sure the oldest girl, Chris, was fed, cared for, and taken to school every day. The baby, Lilly, was taken care of just like she was their very own, so Pam, the mother did not need to worry about her children; she could just be in Houston with Kenneth.

The doctors were not kidding about the severity of this treatment, and it was taking a toll on Kenneth. But he was as cheerful as any child could be, with an attitude that was upbeat and positive, and his appetite was like that of a person twice his size. All of these things were positive, and this was what was needed so that he could endure and continue with this horrific treatment.

I remember one night, it was late, probably around midnight, when Pam called me. She was in tears, and she told me that her son had just convicted her. I inquired what she meant by that statement, and she said, "Kenneth finished his last treatment for the week, and the night after that treatment was always very difficult. He was suffering more than usual and was not sleeping like he normally did." Pam told me she had her head laying on the bed beside Kenneth, talking softly to her Lord, asking why this was happening and asking for something that would give her hope that her son would make it through all of this.

She told me that she felt Kenneth's hand touch the back of her head. She looked up to find Kenneth awake and looking at her. Kenneth then said to his mother, "Don't worry, Mommy. Jesus is here taking care of me, and I will be all right." Then he smiled at her and closed his eyes and went to sleep. Pam told me that she hoped that one day her faith would be as great as that of her son's.

Fortunately for me, I could pray for Pam, and we hung up the phone, then I cried. That night, I know Pam learned what faith can do, and I also experienced a great boost in the faith department as well. I would have loved to have heard Kenneth tell his mother not to worry, that Jesus was there and He was taking care of him, and that he would be fine. I said an additional prayer that night, thanking Jesus for making His presence known to Kenneth and to us through Kenneth, and I also thanked Him for the healing.

The treatments passed, and Kenneth seemed to be doing well, but the day was coming for the tests to be run to see what the status of this leukemia was and if this treatment had been successful. Going through these types of treatments with families, one learns that even though things seem to be working, that is not always the case. It seems sometimes that a person takes two steps forward in the treatments and then takes one, two, or sometimes three steps back. The rollercoaster ride of emotions can be dramatic and very depleting mentally as well as physically and spiritually.

After what seemed like years, in fact, it was just one year, the treatment program came to a final end, and all the scans and tests were performed on Kenneth to see where he was and where the leukemia happened to be if it was there at all. We gathered for the consultation with the doctors, and this time, Kenneth was there to hear the results. The doctors came in, and the file was even thicker than before. The doctors exchanged pleasantries, and they started giving us the news.

At that time, I do not know where Kenneth's parents were mentally, but I had a feeling that Kenneth had already told us the answer. The doctor reviewed every scan and every test and told us that they could not detect any cancer cells anywhere in Kenneth's body. That is when Kenneth put us all to shame when he said, "Remember, Mommy, I told you Jesus was going to make me well." Kenneth, some five plus years later, is as active a young man as any I know, and he still has his tremendous faith in the Lord of lords, Jesus.

DEAD HEART

Every congregation has a lady or ladies who have been part of that congregation for many years and have been regular attenders of the worship services, and they support the church wholly. These ladies can and do become a backbone of the church, preparing meals for families following the loss of loved ones, making sure the church is cleaned, and always ready to help the pastor in any way needed. These ladies will also be at all the church meetings, and they will speak up during those meetings if they believe the conversation is going the wrong way, or the conversation is not needed at all.

Most of these ladies will, from time to time, have health issues, and in the majority of instances, they are very quiet about their health issues, leaving family members or friends to keep the church family up-to-date concerning the latest health information. Most of the time, they just do not think their issue warrants any concern, and in some instances, they just do not want the members of the church to show them any concern. They take an "it-is-nothing-and-it-will-be-all-right attitude."

One of those great ladies developed a heart issue, and no one would have known if it was not for her daughter, Sybil. She kept certain people in the church, including the pastor, informed about what was going on with Beth. Beth had been feeling more exhausted than normal, and she just did not seem to have any energy. At eighty-five, she really did not think too much of this, but this lack of energy and this exhaustion was not like Beth, not like her at all. She was always full of energy and was always doing this and doing that within the community.

Sybil took her to the doctor and a test was run, well, several tests were run, with only one thing standing out. Her blood work came back just as normal as it could be, but the oxygen level in her blood was very low. Further tests were ordered, specifically focused on the lungs and the heart. The lungs came out in top shape, but the heart had a real problem. Beth was sent to a heart specialist in the city, and he proceeded to run more tests based on the results of the preliminary heart test. The results of the test were not good, and he told Beth and her daughter that basically one-third of her heart was not functioning; it was dead.

Beth and her daughter asked for a second opinion concerning this diagnosis, and Beth and her case was referred to a very well-known cardiologist whose offices were located in Houston, Texas. An appointment was made for a Monday mid-morning, and the tests to do a full heart workup were scheduled. That Sunday just before the worship service, Sybil came to me, and we talked about the upcoming cardiologist appointment. Sybil asked me if I would bring her mother forward during the prayers and concerns part of the service, place her in a chair at the front of the sanctuary, invite everyone to come and lay their hands on her, and for me to pray for healing and anoint her mother with oil. I agreed.

Later during the worship service, during the prayers and concern's part, Beth was invited to come forward, which did not sit well with her, and that was because she did not want a fuss made about her and her condition, but she did come forward. Beth took her place in the chair; all were invited to come forward and lay hands on her. Due to the size of the congregation, everyone could not touch Beth, so they touched the person in front of them instead. I prayed to the Lord Jesus, asking for complete healing and for the doctor to come back after the heart work up with good news. I anointed her with oil, and everyone returned to their seats, and the worship service continued.

On Monday, Beth was taken to her cardiologist appointment by her daughter, and the test was performed. On the way to Houston, Beth remarked to her daughter that she did not feel like this special cardiologist would find anything, and she was feeling fine. Sybil took that to mean her mother did not think the results would be any different. After all, one cardiologist is the same as another cardiologist. A simple interview was conducted by one of the cardiologist's associates, and Beth was asked how she was feeling, to which Beth answered, "I haven't felt this good in quite a while."

The heart workup was performed, and the time of waiting ensued. The wait was surprisingly short, only a little over one hour, and they were called in for the results and the consultation. The cardiologist sat down with his associate by his side, and he started with the results of the test. He said, "We could not be happier with the test results because according to what the test proved to us is the fact that there is nothing whatsoever wrong with your heart."

Shock set in with Sybil, and she immediately asked the cardiologist to please explain the result of the test that was previously performed, which showed one-third of her mother's heart was dead. The response from the cardiologist was, "Somehow, the previous test was flawed and inaccurate." At this response, Beth spoke up and said this to the cardiologist, "Let me tell you what happened. My pastor prayed over me, asking the Lord Jesus to heal me, my congregation laid hands on me, and I was anointed with oil. That is what happened. Jesus cured me!"

The cardiologist looked at Beth, and he said, "I have seen this before." One thing about ladies like Beth is they do not hold back when it comes to what they believe happened, especially when it comes to the ability of Jesus.

FAILING MARRIAGE

One thing that is apparent in the United States is the divorce rate, which, depending on which survey you look at, is in excess of fifty percent. So, using fifty percent, that means that one out of every two marriages in the United States fails and winds up in divorce court. Should we be surprised? When one looks at the television, the family, that is husband and wife, is virtually nonexistent. The attack on the family unit is everywhere, and it does not appear to have any change for the better coming anytime soon.

The truly sad fact about divorce is that divorce rates within the Christ-based church mirrors the divorce rate outside the Christ-based church, with those that do not have any church affiliation. So, what is wrong here? Shouldn't divorce rates within those claiming to be Christians and all about following the commands of the Lord be dramatically lower than those of people that openly admit they have nothing to do with the Christ-based church?

I do not know how many matrimonial services I have been involved with, but the thing that gets to me more than people wanting, or claiming to want to get married, are those who want to throw their marriage away over trivial reasons. Years ago, I married a couple, and for this couple, it was neither the bride's nor the groom's first marriage. The groom had been married to his high school sweetheart for over thirty years when, after a three-year bout with cancer, his wife died. The bride had been married to her first husband for over twenty years when he decided he needed to marry a younger woman and so divorce took place.

In this marriage, we have a failed marriage, the bride's, and we have a marriage that lived its full life and was ended by the death of the groom's wife. I was excited for this couple because I knew both of them, and it appeared this marriage would be a great marriage defined by two people who had already experienced marriage in their lives. Both the bride and the groom had children, sons-in-law, and daughters-in-law as well as grandchildren. Both the man and the woman who were about to get married would appear to be solid as the proverbial rock, but were they?

After a short time of marriage, approximately nine months, Max came to me one day, and when he entered my office, I felt like something was wrong, and I was right. Max told me that he and Rita were not happy and that they were both thinking about divorce. Max was not in the mindset of divorce, and he asked me if there was anything that could be done to stop this divorce and correct the situation.

I scheduled a meeting with both of them, and I set these meetings to be on an individual basis, and I would meet with Rita first. Rita came to my office, and my administrative assistant was right across the hall, watching us with the doors open. This was part of the protocol that had been set by the church to protect the pastor and the one being counseled. I asked Rita several questions, the first being, "What are you willing to do to save this marriage?" Her response was not the one I wanted, but at least, she was one hundred percent honest and truthful when she told me she was not sure what she was willing to do to save this marriage. We continued with the question-and-answer session, and after about one hour, we concluded our meeting, and I had my notes.

The next meeting was between Max and me, and when I asked Max what he was willing to do to save this marriage, he told me, "I am willing to do whatever it takes to save this marriage, and I think we are where we are because of me. It is my fault." For everyone that has ever worked with a married couple with problems, this response by Max was totally unexpected. I wanted to hear he was willing to do whatever it would take to save the marriage, but I did not expect to get at the root problem on the first session.

I set up another session with Max, and I called Rita to get her back in so we could discuss what Max had told me. Rita arrived, and we exchanged pleasantries, we said a prayer, and we started discussing what I had learned from Max. It was obvious that Rita loved Max and loved him as much as any wife could love her husband, and she told me she never thought Max would admit to his problems. She told me where she was willing to meet Max, but she did say she could not take the verbal abuse anymore. I told her she should not have to endure it anymore and that Max had agreed to change, but he would need time and help.

Max came for his next session, and we discussed his issues and problems he had with Rita. You probably think that Rita had some real quirky attributes about her, and if you thought that, you are wrong. The issues were that Max had been very happily married to his first wife for over thirty years, and if cancer had not cut that marriage short, he would still be married to his first wife, his first love, his high school sweetheart.

Max had been the center of his family. Everything in his family revolved around the decisions he made for that family, and those decisions were good, sound biblical decisions. But now what had happened was that there were two different families trying to operate as one, and Max still thought he should make all the decisions for this new combined family. The problem was that Rita and her children, daughter-in-law, and grandchildren looked to her son for leadership, and her son's views and Max's views differed on some things, so there was a problem. Rita defended her son, and Max defended his position as head of the household.

Some compromises had to be worked out so Max, Rita, and I decided to have a new family meeting and discuss the future of Max and Rita's marriage. I contacted all the family members on both sides, set a date for the meeting, worked with Rita and Max concerning the food, and we were hopefully set. The day of the meeting came, and all were there, but I could tell the children on both sides were somewhat nervous and not really being themselves.

I knew Max's children, so I started with them and explained Max and Rita's situation. I took the Bible, and I read where the man is to be the head of the household, and then I turned to Rita's son, Mark. I asked if he thought that Max was or could be a great husband for his mother and if he felt like he could allow Max to be the center of the newly formed blended family. Mark smiled, got up out of his chair, walked across the room to Max, and apologized for his behavior. Max stood up and did the same with Mark; they shook hands, then hugged, and the meal was a great success.

I continued to meet with Max and Rita for almost one year on a regular basis. We would discuss any and all issues that had arisen since the last meeting, decide how to move forward, and then we would join hands and pray. Max and Rita became great students of the Bible, and they worked together teaching each other the Scripture. Their marriage was in trouble, but because Max realized what he had and the fact that he did not want to lose it, the marriage worked.

In all great marriages, there is a man and a woman who love the other more than they are loved in return. They constantly talk about all the things, good and bad, that happen in their marriage, and then they spend time together in the presence of their Lord and Savior, Jesus the Christ. If all marriages would do those things, I believe divorce, especially among those in the Christ-based church, would virtually come to an end.

HURTING WRISTS

Several years ago, right after I retired from full-time ministry and moved to our current home about sixty miles north of Houston, in an area that I really did not think I would be able to live in, but for my wife and I (both of us like to play golf), this was a great place, and we found a home right on one of the golf courses. We have a great view of part of a par 5, so we get to see many golfers come by our home each day of the year. This area also has an abundant population of white-tailed deer, and they come right up in our backyard, looking for something to eat.

From day to day, I noticed a man playing golf on a regular basis, and he was playing alone as much was he was playing with partners. I learned that it was not that he could not find anyone to play golf with; it was just that he played every day. One day, he was playing on the hole we live on, and he hit a shot that wound up close to being in our backyard. We were sitting on our patio, enjoying the day, when Larry pulled up looking for his golf ball. We pointed out where it was, and I walked out and introduced myself and my wife, and I told Larry I had noticed that he played almost every day.

He told me that if he was up and able, he would be out on the courses playing. I gave him one of my cards and told him that I was basically retired except for Sundays, and if he needed a playing partner, I would be available. Larry took my card, and I wondered if he would ever contact me since my card plainly stated that I was a minister. Some people get a little nervous about playing with a preacher, but in a few days, very few days, Larry called one morning and wanted to know if I would be interested in playing with him, and the tee time was eleven o'clock that morning. My response was a definite "Yes!"

I went down to the club house and went to the warm-up area and started to warm up before going to meet Larry at the number one tee. When I arrived at the first tee, Larry was just pulling up in his cart, and we exchanged pleasantries, and then he told me I could tee off first. I walked up to the tee and stuck my tee in the ground, placed my golf ball on top of it, and prepared to hit my first drive. For those of you who play this game of golf, you know too well about the first tee, especially when you are playing with someone for the very first time.

The drive went exceptionally well. Larry hit his tee shot, and we were both in the fairway, the short grass as it is called, and we were off for about four hours of golf on a day that could not have been more beautiful. Along about the third or fourth tee box, Larry spoke up and told me that he noticed by my card that I was a minister. He questioned the card because on one side listed one church and on the other side listed another church, so I told him that I had retired from full-time ministry, but I was serving two small rural country churches as their pastor on Sunday. I explained that I had no real duties the rest of the week, but Sunday, I would be at one of those churches, leading the worship service, and this way, with one church on one side and the other church on the reverse side, I only needed one card.

Larry told me that he did not go to church. He told me that he worshipped the Lord out here on the golf course in the middle of nature. My response to Larry was one I do not think he expected from a preacher, but I told him this was as beautiful a place as I knew to worship the Lord, and we continued playing the rest of the round. At the end of the round, we went to the club house, and downstairs, there is little snack bar, so we went in, and Larry had a bottle of tea, and I had a Coke.

It seemed like we played on a regular basis for a good while, and I learned a good bit about Larry and his family. Larry's wife was a woman of great faith, and she was involved with her church and virtually never missed worship services on Sunday morning while Larry played golf. Not too many weeks or months went by, and Larry invited me to play with him and a man called Ward. Ward had owned a very prosperous business in the area but had since sold it to his children, and they were operating it successfully. Ward now played golf.

Ward was a retired man about my age, and I learned that he was the director of the local men's ecumenical choir, and Larry was a member of that choir. This men's choir would go around the area performing in various churches throughout the week, not every week, but normally at least once a month, with the Easter and Christmas holidays a busy time for this choir. Ward invited me to come the next week to hear them at one of the local churches. I accepted his invitation, and we went. We had a wonderful evening, and the choir was great.

Weeks went by, and once again Ward joined us, but this time, the Lord started working. Ward asked Larry if he could understand why the Lord was after him since he was part of the men's choir and now, he was playing golf with a minister. Larry just laughed and made a statement to the effect that he really did not know why the Lord was doing what He was doing? We had a great day playing, and Larry told me that on Saturday morning, he had put together a group to play, and I was included, along with the president of one of the local banks. I looked forward to that Saturday and the opportunity to meet this president of the local bank.

The Saturday came, and when we arrived at the club house, I noticed Larry talking to a man who was getting his clubs out of his trunk, and I assumed this was the bank president. I drove over, and Larry introduced me to George. He was indeed the president of the local bank. George said he was going to go rent a cart and then warm up just a bit, and he would be ready to play. I told George that if he did not mind riding with a preacher, he was welcome to share my cart. He accepted my offer, so off we went to warm up a bit.

That day was great, and George told me to call him if I had any openings on any day I was going to play and that he would love to join me and my group. I knew that I did not want to move in on Larry's banker, but if Larry and I were not playing and he had not invited George, then I would feel free to invite him to play. I did that on several occasions, with George and I sharing my cart to play eighteen holes together.

One day, while Larry and I were playing, he came to me on the last hole and inquired about my two churches. I explained how the system of rotating from one church on Sunday to the other church on the next Sunday worked and told him which church we would be serving that coming Sunday. I really did not have any expectations concerning Larry and his wife coming to worship with us. For these few months, Larry and I had many discussions concerning church, the Bible, the Lord, and my positions on numerous subjects, and I really enjoyed those conversations.

Sunday came, and lo and behold, Larry and his wife walked into the church a few minutes before we were to get started with the worship service. I introduced him to several of the members, and the worship service proceeded. At the end of the service, Larry told me that the men's choir was going to perform at a local church in our hometown that evening, so I told him we would be there. When I told my wife of our new plans for that Sunday evening, she was as excited as I was because we really enjoyed the men's choir and their music.

We arrived at the local church, and we walked into the sanctuary. Walking down the center isle of the sanctuary, at about halfway, or a little less, a woman's voice called out my name, and when I turned, it as Larry's wife, Linda. She invited us to sit with her, and we took our place in the pew beside her. Linda looked at me, and her eyes filled with tears, and she said, "I want to thank you from the bottom of my heart for getting my husband in church. He has not been in church for over twenty-five years. I do not know what you did, but I thank you."

I immediately told Linda that she did not need to thank me because I had done nothing to get Larry in church. I told her the one she must thank was the Lord. I told her the Lord placed me in the position I had with Larry and that I really never brought up him coming to church even though we had many discussions about church, the Bible, and the Lord. The evening was great, and after the performance, I spoke to Ward. Then Larry, Linda, my wife, and I went to get something to eat.

Larry and Linda became regulars at the worship services at both churches, and they even became involved in the adult Sunday school class. During my preaching, I would speak about the power of prayer and that Jesus told his disciples that they would do greater things than He did while He was here on earth. I would tell the congregation that we accomplish great things through prayer and our actions and godly deeds and behavior.

One day, Larry was having some problems with his wrists during the day of golf, and on the last hole, he came over to my cart and he asked me, "Do you really think prayer works?" That was a great question, but I was not sure where Larry was headed, but my response was that I totally believed prayer worked. Larry told me he was having trouble with his left or lead wrist, and it was really causing him trouble, and he wanted to know if I would say a prayer for healing of his wrist.

I got out of my cart and took a step or two toward Larry, sticking out my hands, and told him, "Let's pray for healing!" We joined hands right there at the end of the eighteenth hole. I prayed to the Lord, asking him to heal Larry's wrist and to make him well. When we look in the Scripture at the meaning of the word *well,* the way it is used, it means physical and spiritual wholeness. When Jesus healed someone, it is said that he made them "well."

That next Sunday, we did not see Larry and Linda in church, but he told me they would be down at the beach that weekend and that we would not see them in church. Larry called me late the next week and wanted to play golf. He acquired a tee time, and we met to go play. We played the eighteen holes, and we wound up on the same last hole where Larry had asked me to pray for his wrist. When we finished, Larry came up to me after finishing while we were walking off the green and he told me, "Your prayer worked, and my wrist was totally healed.",

Larry and Linda are still active in the churches, and we always look forward to seeing them in church, and we still play on a regular basis, with Larry asking for prayers for various things but most of them now are for other players he knows with problems, and the Lord has continued to display His power He has given to us through prayer.

THE RETURN OF THROAT CANCER

Throughout my time in ministry and the vast numbers of people I have dealt with who have suffered through cancer and cancer treatment to be deemed cancer-free, is a rather large group. One of the things I have learned is the fact that it makes a great difference in the outcome of one's cancer treatment is the choice that person makes concerning where they will go for treatment, especially their initial treatment. There are untold places in this country that are set up to treat cancer, but there are few that are truly cancer research treatment centers. Consequently, I believe that far too many people lose their battle with cancer because they went to the wrong place first.

Another thing I have learned when it comes to people who have endured cancer treatment and have been given the great news that their cancer is in remission, undetectable within their body, or are deemed to be cured is that these survivors knew it was back, as they, one after another, when they or if they have had a relapse or reoccurrence of this disease, have told me. There is just something about this disease that a person who has been through it knows this disease, and I feel they connect some way with this thing that can reoccur and come back to torture them once again.

You have learned from my writing that it makes me no difference who a person happens to be, whether that person is part of the churches I serve, or if they are just someone I know or who is pointed out to me who has a problem where the Lord needs to be brought into the equation. Such is the case with Jim and his wife, Mary. Jim and Mary had been through a long multiyear battle with throat cancer suffered by Jim. First thing that usually comes to mind is the question, "Did Jim smoke?" The answer to that question is no, he never did smoke or use any form of tobacco products during his life leading up to his diagnosis of throat cancer.

Jim was diagnosed, and the treatment started. I do not know the pain, the devastation to his body, or the mental strain that took place during Jim's treatment because I did not know him or his wife at that time. All I know is that the treatment was not quick, and it took more than one year of treatment before he was able to "ring out" and feel good about being finished with the treatments and being cancer-free.

A couple of years later, I met Jim and his wife, Mary, and they became good friends with us. Jim and I played golf together. We went out to eat together with all of us really enjoying one particular local family-owned Mexican food restaurant. One day, I noticed Jim and his wife together, sitting outside in the morning, and I could tell that they were in the middle of a difficult discussion. What it was I had no idea, but I just felt the Lord pulling me to them to find out what they needed.

When I arrived at their patio table, the mood was very serious, and I could tell they were being drawn together because of some sort of real problem or situation. I sat down and inquired if there was anything I could do? Mary excused herself and went into the house. I felt she needed to be away for a few moments, leaving Jim and I alone at the table on their patio. Jim told me of the problem he was having, and it was his throat. He told me that he was going to see a doctor and that he was returning to the cancer facility the following week for a complete workup.

Jim was certain that the cancer he had battled and thought he had defeated was back. Like I just said, I do not know how cancer survivors know when their cancer returns, but I am convinced they know and according to Jim, he knew it was back. I could tell that he was shaken, and I could tell he did not want to go through this again.

This was happening on a Wednesday or a Thursday, and his appointment with the local doctor was that very day, with the appointment at his cancer facility in Houston the following week around the middle of the week. I looked at Jim. I could see what I felt like was fear in his eyes, and I asked him if he would like for me to pray for him for healing, comfort, and peace. His response was positive, and we joined hands, and I prayed to our Lord Jesus to come and be with Jim, granting him comfort from the pain, peace, knowing Jesus was with him, and for complete healing of this thing in his neck and throat area.

The appointment with his local doctor went the way one would expect, and his doctor was informed that the following week, Jim would be going to Houston for a complete workup on his throat at the cancer hospital there. It is my information that his local doctor told him that was a very smart idea. I do not really know how to process what his doctor told him, but I do not feel it made Jim feel any better. In fact, I feel like he felt even more fear.

I did not see Jim or Mary before the appointment and the workup on Jim's neck and throat, so I did not know what had transpired. After the appointment, Jim and Mary came home, and they asked to come over to our house to talk to us. There was not a long time in between the call wanting to come over and them arriving, but it seemed like a small eternity. When Jim and Mary came in, Jim was smiling, Mary was laughing, so I took that as good news.

We sat down, and Jim proceeded to go over what had happened to him since our prayer time on his patio. He told me he did not know what I had done, but before he arrived at his appointment in Houston, all the swelling, all the pain, all the feeling the cancer was back was gone. The doctors in Houston ran the tests and the scans but could find absolutely nothing anywhere. Jim told me that he knew his cancer was back but that my prayer, he was sure, had taken it away.

I believe in the power of prayer, but I believe even more in the healing power of our Lord Jesus. I have seen it too many times not to believe in His power. Was Jim's cancer back in his throat? I do not know the answer to that, but like I said, people who go through cancer and the treatment associated with their particular cancer have an uncanny sense if and when that cancer returns. Jim said it returned, and that's enough for me. Jim told me the prayer that I prayed that morning on his patio took the cancer away. That's enough for me because I know the power of healing our Lord has, and I know how He answers prayers!

PERSONAL LOSS AND BRAIN ANEURYSM AND SALVATION

Let me tell you about some personal things that have happened to me in my life. Some people have the idea that preachers and their families are somehow exempt from the things of this life. Let me tell you that I am walking through this world just like anyone else, with one exception—I am walking shoulder to shoulder with my Lord and Savior Jesus. He is right there with me through everything I experience in this life no matter what it happens to be.

I have gone through the loss of my grandparents on both sides, the loss of my mother and father, the loss of my wife's parents, so loss is something we all go through, but I feel fortunate to have never had to go through a loss without my Lord Jesus with me. Possibly to date, the toughest loss was our granddaughter a couple of years ago to breast cancer. Today, in this country, I feel the medical profession can detect any disease, and if detected early enough, they can treat it successfully. The problem comes in the early detection. Too often, we as human beings do not do our part to check ourselves and when we find something that is not normal, then we need to get to a doctor and hopefully they will come to the proper diagnosis.

The biggest problem for me is that since I deal with so many other people's problems and losses, sometimes it takes a little bit for my personal loss to sink in and for me to go through a proper grieving process for myself, and that is important. How we deal with loss is, I believe, a very personal thing, and I do not believe it can be written down in a book with five or six or seven steps telling us this is how it happens because all too often, the grief process does not follow the book.

When my wife and I attended the final service of our granddaughter, it was a time filled with grief for everyone there including myself, but since I am a pastor, people looked to me for answers and to see how I would handle this loss. I do not know what they expect or if what they see in my reactions or actions meets with their approval or not, but it was what it was.

A short time later, a few months, we received a call from our oldest daughter concerning her husband. He had gone to work that morning, but during the morning, he had been found on the floor of the room he was working in, and he was not conscious. He was transported to a local hospital, and they discovered that he had suffered a massive brain aneurysm, and there was nothing that could be done for him. Because of this, he did not survive, and our daughter suffered a major loss, and so did we, but this was the love of her life, and we were five hundred miles away, trying to help her over the phone.

The time came, and we were going to travel to our daughter's, and I would be the one officiating the final celebration of our son-in-law's life. One thing that is best for a preacher is to not do close family end-of-life services because it is very difficult to separate yourself from your loved one and make it through the service without losing it emotionally. The day went as well as could be expected, and a couple of days later, we returned home.

Once we arrived home, that was when I went through my deep grieving process, grieving for the loss of my son-in-law, who made my daughter extremely happy, but also trying to figure out how to help my daughter through this time of loss, being that I was five hundred miles away from her. That meant I could not hold her in my arms and say the things one would say to his daughter during a time like this.

Time has continued to march on, and over the past two years, healing has taken place. Not total healing, but healing is taking place, and I know it will continue to progress, and we will look forward to other things in the future. That is another thing I love about faith and especially faith in the Lord Jesus; it gives all of us a future, a future we can look forward to even though we are not sure what lies ahead while on this earth.

The biggest thing I think about and strive for is to try and help people realize the importance of a personal relationship with the Son of God, Jesus. The Lord wants all of His ultimate creation, mankind, to be in eternity with Him; we call it heaven. I believe that from the time we are born to the time we leave this world, our Lord is with us. That part of the Lord is called the Holy Spirit. So no matter what chronological age we happen to be, we have the grace of God with us. At some point, that point being different for every individual, we must come to the realization that we cannot make it through this life, this world, alone; and we need help. We must realize that we need a savior, and that savior is Jesus the Christ.

Once we have made that decision, we need to follow the process within the Scripture, and we need to accept Jesus as the risen Son of God. Once we have made that heartfelt decision, then we need to ask for help in leading our lives and living according to all the commands laid out for us in the Bible. This is the tough part because we have just embarked on a lifelong journey with the Lord. We will falter or fail and need the grace of forgiveness, and we will need to strive with all our might to live a life that glorifies our Lord.

By doing this, we are granted our free gift of salvation; it is a free gift, but like all gifts, we cannot earn it through the things or works we do. It is through faith that we are saved. My desire for everyone, including all of my family, is that everyone takes advantage of that free gift, and by doing so, we will receive eternal life. Like the old hymn says, "When we all get to heaven, what a glorious day that will be!" That is when we will get to see all of our friends and loved ones who accepted the free gift of eternal life or salvation.

In closing, I just need to tell you there are many more stories, but like John in his gospel, I could not include all of them, or I would never finish writing this piece. May God bless you and keep you, and always go to the Lord in prayer when you need help of any kind. Go there as a first action and not as a last resort. The Lord is waiting to hear your prayers!

ABOUT THE AUTHOR

John Burchell was born in Kansas in 1947, and shortly after his birth, his mother divorced his father, but in about four years, she remarried. He was raised by his stepfather and mother in Kansas, went through the public-school system, graduated high school, and went on to attend college on an athletic scholarship to play football. After college, he went to work for an automotive manufacturer, and during that time, he met his wife, and they were married. He spent a good part of his working life in the automotive industry but ultimately found his Lord Jesus, and that changed his entire life as well as his career path. He made the decision to enter the ministry with the help of his wife and many supporters. He attended seminary and ultimately was appointed as a full-time pastor of a small Northeast Texas church. After many years in the ministry, he decided to retire from the full-time ministry but still serves two small churches as their pastor during his retirement and is still serving those churches today as their pastor.